To:

_____

From:

_____

Promises to Encourage Your Soul

Inspirational Refreshment for Your Spirit

BARBOUR
PUBLISHING

© 2012 by Barbour Publishing, Inc.

Print ISBN 978-1-61626-937-1

eBook Editions:
Adobe Digital Edition (.epub) 978-1-62029-626-4
Kindle and MobiPocket Edition (.prc) 978-1-62029-625-7

Devotional readings are from *365 Daily Whispers of Wisdom for Busy Women*, published by Barbour Publishing, Inc.

Prayers by Jackie M. Johnson are from *Power Prayers for Women*, published by Barbour Publishing, Inc.

Prayers by Donna K. Maltese are from *Power Prayers to Start Your Day*, published by Barbour Publishing, Inc.

Scripture quotations marked KJV are taken from the King James Version of the Bible.

Scripture quotations marked NIV are taken from the HOLY BIBLE, NEW INTERNATIONAL VERSION®. NIV®. Copyright © 1973, 1978, 1984, 2011 by Biblica, Inc.™ Used by permission. All rights reserved worldwide.

Scripture quotations marked NKJV are taken from the New King James Version. Copyright © 1982 by Thomas Nelson, Inc. Used by permission. All rights reserved.

Scripture quotations marked NASB are taken from the New American Standard Bible, © 1960, 1962, 1963, 1968, 1971, 1972, 1973, 1975, 1977, 1995 by The Lockman Foundation. Used by permission.

Scripture quotations marked NLT are taken from the HOLY BIBLE, New Living Translation, copyright © 1996, 2004, 2007. Used by permission of Tyndale House Publishers, Inc. Carol Stream, Illinois 60188. All rights reserved.

Scripture quotations marked MSG are from *THE MESSAGE*. Copyright © by Eugene H. Peterson 1993, 1994, 1995, 1996, 2000, 2001, 2002. Used by permission of NavPress Publishing Group.

Cover design by Kirk DouPonce, DogEared Design

Published by Barbour Publishing, Inc., P.O. Box 719, Uhrichsville, Ohio 44683, www.barbourbooks.com

Our mission is to publish and distribute inspirational products offering exceptional value and biblical encouragement to the masses.

Member of the
Evangelical Christian
Publishers Association

Printed in China.

Contents

Introduction

Be Encouraged!

May our Lord Jesus Christ himself and God our Father. . .encourage your hearts and strengthen you.

2 THESSALONIANS 2:16–17 NIV

Some days we need a gentle hand to pick us up and a voice to whisper encouragement in our ears. Life can be challenging, and when trials come our way, we may feel discouraged. But God does not fail us, no matter what our days hold. His Word provides comfort for all our troubles.

Blessings

"Blessed be the name of God forever and ever,

for wisdom and might are His."

DANIEL 2:20 NKJV

Mary's Song of Praise

Lord, of all the women in the world—young or old, rich or poor, of high status or low—You chose a young girl from an unimportant, backwater province to bear Your Son, our Savior. Her response was, appropriately, a song of joy and praise, one of the most moving prayers in the Bible. Mary understood that You had given her a great honor that would be remembered forever, and she welcomed it—as well as the responsibility that came with it—with joy. You bless my life in many ways every day, Father. May I receive Your blessings with a song of thanksgiving on my lips.

—Toni Sortor

Unappreciated Blessings?

When God brings us through a trial, do we worship Him with great thankfulness, or do we take that blessing as our due? Though God is great, He doesn't appreciate being taken for granted any more than we would.

Required to describe King Nebuchadnezzar's bad dream to him or face imminent death, Daniel didn't worry or have a pity party. Instead, he called a prayer meeting of his three best friends. In the middle of the night, God answered their prayers, revealing Nebuchadnezzar's dream to Daniel, the wisest of the Babylonian king's wise men.

Daniel's first and very grateful response, in the midst of his relief, was to praise the Lord who had saved his life. He gave God recognition for His saving grace even before he went to see the king who had threatened to kill him.

We may believe that our Lord answers in such life-and-death situations, but do we have confidence He takes care of smaller troubles, too? And when He does respond to an ordinary situation, do we give thanks?

— Pamela McQuade

When we lose one blessing,

another is often most unexpectedly

given in its place.

— C. S. Lewis

"I am coming to you now, but I say these things
while I am still in the world, so that they may have
the full measure of my joy within them."

JOHN 17:13 NIV

Enjoying God's Blessings

Lord, I thank You for the work of Your hands. A wildflower, a mountain scene, the ocean waves on a white sand beach—the beauty of the earth reveals Your glory. Thank You for the smile of a child, the touch of my beloved's hand, the warmth of our home. I am grateful for the love of friends and meaningful work. You have done great things for us, and we are filled with joy. Thank You for Your many blessings.

—Jackie M. Johnson

God be merciful to us and bless us,
and cause His face to shine upon us.

Never lose an opportunity of seeing anything

that is beautiful; for beauty is God's handwriting—

a wayside sacrament. Welcome it in every fair face,

in every fair sky, in every fair flower,

and thank God for it as a cup of blessing.

—Ralph Waldo Emerson

For he that is mighty hath done to me
great things; and holy is his name.
And his mercy is on them that fear him
from generation to generation.

LUKE 1:49–50 KJV

Just Half a Cup

"Just half a cup, please." A friend is offered a cup of piping hot coffee, but she declines a full cup, accepting only a small amount. Perhaps she is trying to be polite, or maybe she feels as though she's had enough coffee already that day. But it is difficult and unnatural for her friend to stop pouring at half a cup, so she pours just a bit more than what was requested. She wants to give her friend the fullest possible measure of enjoyment that she can in that one cup of coffee.

That's how our Father feels when He longs to bestow His richest blessings and wisdom on us. He loves us, so He desires to fill our cup to overflowing with the things that He knows will bring us pleasure and growth. Do you tell Him to stop pouring when your cup is only half full? You may not even realize it, but perhaps your actions dictate that your cup remain half empty. Seek a full cup and enjoy the full measure of the joy of the Lord.

—Nicole O'Dell

Joy in Giving

Lord, I thank You for Your blessings. Whether in plenty or with little, I want to be a cheerful giver. I desire to give from a full heart that serves, not reluctantly or with complaining. I long to see Your money used in ways that will bless others—through my tithing at church, giving to mission organizations, or helping the needy. I choose to give at whatever level I can—and ask You to bless it.

—Jackie M. Johnson

Scripture again and again

points to God the Father

as the headwaters of a constant

stream of blessing for us.

— Bill Gothard

As having nothing, and yet possessing all things.

2 CORINTHIANS 6:10 KJV

A Blessing of Peace

Lord, long ago You told Moses to have Aaron and his sons bless the Israelites with these words. I ask that You would bless me with peace as I pray: "The LORD bless you and keep you; the LORD make his face shine upon you and be gracious to you; the LORD turn his face toward you and give you peace." Turn to me, and let Your love and mercy shine on me so I can be a light that shines the way for others.

—Jackie M. Johnson

Contagious Laughter

Nothing brings more joy to our hearts than when God blesses our lives. Like Sarah, we may at first laugh with disbelief when God promises us our heart's desire. For some reason, we doubt that He can do what we deem impossible. Yet God asks us, as He did Sarah, "Is anything too hard for the LORD?" (Genesis 18:14 NKJV).

Then when the blessings shower down upon us, we overflow with joy. Everything seems bright and right with the world. With God, the impossible has become a reality. We bubble over with laughter, and when we laugh, the world laughs with us! It's contagious!

When Satan bombards us with lies—"God's not

real"; "You'll never get that job"; "Mr. Right? He'll never come along"—it's time to look back at God's Word and remember Sarah. Embed in your mind the truth that with God, nothing is impossible (see Matthew 19:26). And then, in the midst of the storm, in the darkness of night, in the crux of the trial, laugh, letting the joy of God's truth be your strength.

—Donna K. Maltese

Comfort
&
Contentment

But godliness with contentment is great gain.

1 TIMOTHY 6:6 KJV

Covetousness

It is so easy to fall into the trap of covetousness, Lord. Today everything is bigger, better, new and improved. About the only thing that doesn't get repackaged every year is Ivory soap, but that still gets me clean. I miss old-fashioned contentment, using time-proven products, and watching the sun set instead of the evening news. Still, I admit I am not totally content. There's just so much available, and some of it looks pretty good. On days when a commercial gets to me a little, remind me that I have everything I really need, Lord. Best of all, I have You, whose promises never change, and You will always supply my true needs.

—Toni Sortor

Contentment in Christ

In the midst of a conversation, the young woman was caught short.

"Will you ever be content?" her friend asked.

"I don't know," she said. "I don't think so. I always want things to be better than they are."

The question echoed as the years passed. A career melted into marriage and motherhood. With each challenge, she worked harder to make things better. Nevertheless, she often felt empty. She wondered if there was a better way to live.

There is. True profit and gain lie not in toiling for money, but in being content with one's situation.

How can we learn contentment?

We must start looking to Jesus. If we take hold of

all we have as joint heirs with Christ and as partakers of grace, we will have no desire for the world's riches.

According to the Bible, we are raised up with Jesus and are seated in the heavenly places with Him. We have His constant presence through the indwelling Holy Spirit. He has given us all things that pertain unto life and godliness. What more do we need?

We need a fresh vision for who we are in Christ. Therein we will find contentment.

—Helen Middlebrooke

The thought of You stirs us so deeply that we

cannot be content unless we praise You,

because You have made us for Yourself,

and our hearts find no peace until they rest in You.

—Saint Augustine

She thought, "If I just touch his clothes, I will be healed."

MARK 5:28 NIV

Finding Contentment

Lord, please help me to find my contentment in You.
I don't want to be defined by "stuff"—the things I
own or what I do. May my greatest happiness in life
be knowing who You are and who I am in Christ. May
I treasure the simple things in life, those things that
bring me peace. With Your grace, I rest secure. Like
Mary, I choose to sit at Your feet. You, Lord, are my
satisfaction.

—Jackie M. Johnson

For we brought nothing into this world,

and it is certain we can carry nothing out.

And having food and clothing,

with these we shall be content.

1 TIMOTHY 6:7—8 NKJV

God is everything that is good and comfortable for us.

He is our clothing that for love wraps us, clasps us,

and all surrounds us for tender love.

—Julian of Norwich

Be content with such things as ye have: for he hath said,

I will never leave thee, nor forsake thee.

HEBREWS 13:5 KJV

Reach Out and Touch

We should never underestimate the power of touch. In our busy lives, as we rush from one appointment to another, skimping on affection with our families and loved ones can become routine. We wave good-bye to our children without stopping for a hug. Husbands head off to work with the barest brush of a kiss.

We do our loved ones a disservice, however, when we skip touching them. Touching communicates our affection but also our affirmation and sympathy. You can encourage people—or comfort them—with a simple touch. The Bible records Jesus touching many people, comforting and healing them. He also let people touch Him, such as the sinful woman who touched and kissed His feet (Luke 7:38).

In Mark 5, however, the true power of a simple touch is beautifully portrayed. This woman who had suffered for so long believed so strongly in Jesus that she knew the quickest touch of His hem would heal her. She reached out, and her faith made her well.

So hold those you love close. Hug them, and let them see a bit of Jesus' love in you every day.

—Ramona Richards

Affliction

I have been afflicted in my lifetime, as have most women, but You helped me walk out of affliction and invited me to Your continual feast. Right now I am still at Your banquet, but I know affliction will come again. I am content and comfortable, enjoying life to its fullest. I don't know if I will feel that way when trials come to me again, because I don't really have a merry heart. Like most people, I am happiest when things are going nicely, but when things go wrong, my heart is not so merry. Help me get over this nagging self-doubt, Father. Remind me that Your blessings are forever and I have nothing to fear. Give me a merry heart, I pray.

—Toni Sortor

God doesn't comfort us to make us comfortable,

but to make us comforters.

— Billy Graham

Praise be to the God and Father of our Lord Jesus Christ,

the Father of compassion and the God of all comfort,

who comforts us in all our troubles,

so that we can comfort those in any trouble

with the comfort we ourselves receive from God.

2 CORINTHIANS 1:3–4 NIV

God Is Your Comfort

Lord, there is none like You. When I am sad, You are my comfort. Your calm presence restores my soul. Your words are cool, refreshing water to my spirit. Despite my confusion, You guide me in paths of righteousness, and it's all for Your glory. Even when I feel like I'm lost in a dark valley, I will not be afraid— for You are with me. Your gentle strength and Your divine authority comfort me.

—Jackie M. Johnson

What Next?

Have you ever had a day when everything has gone wrong? The neighbor's dogs bark all night, so you don't get any sleep. You spill coffee on your favorite blouse. The car has a flat tire. You're running late, so you get a ticket for speeding. You end up wondering what next—what else can go wrong?

On days like this it's hard to find any reason to be joyful. How can we be happy when every time we turn around another disaster strikes? Instead of greeting everyone with a smile, on these down days we tend to be cranky or snarly. We tell anyone willing to listen about our terrible lot in life.

Rejoicing in the Lord is not a matter of circumstances but of will. We can choose to remember the

God of our salvation and be content with His love for us. No matter how much goes awry, we have so much more to be thankful for because of the grace of God.

God is sovereign. With His help we can rise above the worry of our circumstances to find peace and contentment. Then, no matter what is happening in our lives, other people will see the joy of God.

—Nancy Farrier

Hope

I pray that God, the source of hope,
will fill you completely with joy and peace
because you trust in him.
Then you will overflow with confident hope
through the power of the Holy Spirit.

Romans 15:13 NLT

Anxiety

Generalized anxiety, the doctors call it—that nagging feeling that something is wrong but cannot be pinned down. A lot of women know this feeling. It seems to be our job to worry about others and see dangers others never glimpse. Yet You did not create me to live in fear, but in hope. It is Your joy to watch over me. Who could do it better? You are with my husband on the long drive to work. You hold my child's hand at the crosswalk. I am not responsible for everyone and everything—You are, and I know You are trustworthy. Help me to hope in You and trust Your protection.

—Toni Sortor

God of Hope

In our busy, fast-paced lives, we may feel exhausted at times. Our culture fosters frenzy and ignores the need for rest and restoration. Constantly putting out fires and completing tasks, working incessantly, we may feel discouraged and disheartened with life. There is more to life than this, isn't there?

Our God of hope says, "Yes!" God desires to fill us to the brim with joy and peace. But to receive this gladness, rest, and tranquillity, we need to have faith in the God who is trustworthy and who says, "Anything is possible if a person believes" (Mark 9:23 NLT). We need to place our confidence in God who, in His timing and through us, will complete that task, mend that relationship, or do whatever it is we need.

The key to receiving and living a life of hope, joy, and peace is recounting God's faithfulness out loud, quietly in your heart, and to others. When you begin to feel discouraged, exhausted, and at the end of your rope, stop; go before the throne of grace and recall God's faithfulness.

—Tina C. Elacqua

We walk without fear, full of hope and courage

and strength to do His will, waiting for the endless

good which He is always giving as fast as

He can get us able to take it in.

— George MacDonald

Keep your eyes on Jesus, who both began and finished this race we're in.

HEBREWS 12:2 MSG

Hopeful Surety

Although I cannot see or touch You, Lord, You are here with me. You are waiting to hear my prayer, ready to do what's best for me. You know me better than I know myself. Thank You for spending these precious moments here with me as I open my heart and share my hopes, dreams, fears, and needs with You. Increase my faith as I hope in You.

—Donna K. Maltese

But I will hope continually,
and will praise You yet more and more.

PSALM 71:14 NKJV

Life is what we are alive to. It is not length but breadth. . . . Be alive to. . .goodness, kindness, purity, love, history, poetry, music, flowers, stars, God, and eternal hope.

— Maltbie D. Babcock

Why art thou cast down, O my soul?

and why art thou disquieted within me?

hope thou in God: for I shall yet praise him,

who is the health of my countenance, and my God.

PSALM 42:11 KJV

Remember This

It can happen in a split second. Your life is suddenly turned upside down. Your mother is rushed to the emergency room. Your doctor utters the word "cancer." Layoffs leave you jobless. Dark clouds quickly obscure your vision. Emotions reel out of control. Questions without answers rush through your mind. Life has been dramatically altered in the blink of an eye.

If you have not encountered such an experience, it's likely that someday you will. Prepare yourself now. Remember that when life throws us curveballs, we may be caught off guard, but God never is. He knows all things: past, present, and future. Since He knows what lies ahead, He can safely navigate us through the chaos.

When our heads are spinning and tears are flowing, there is only one thing to remember: Focus on Jesus. He will never leave you nor forsake you. When you focus on Him, His presence envelops you. Where there is despair, He imparts hope. Where there is fear, He imparts faith. Where there is worry, He imparts peace. He will lead you on the right path and grant you wisdom for the journey. When the unexpected trials of life come upon you, remember this: Focus on Jesus.

—Julie Rayburn

Holding on to Hope

Lord, please help me hold on to hope. Sustain me according to Your promises. Abraham had great faith in You, Lord, and became the father of many nations— just as You had promised him. Even though he was old, You provided a baby boy for him and his wife, Sarah. As You did for them, Lord, please fulfill my longings— and Your vision for my life's purpose.

—Jackie M. Johnson

To lose hope has the same effect on our heart

as it would be to stop breathing.

— Brent Curtis

But if we hope for that we see not,

then do we with patience wait for it.

ROMANS 8:25 KJV

Always Have Hope

Lord, please help me look forward with a positive attitude—with faith, not fear. Anchor me with hope for my soul, firm and secure. Captain the craft of my life, and keep me from wandering into doubt and insecurity over the future. I thank You, Lord, that You are in control!

—Jackie M. Johnson

Get Moving!

Feeling run down? Has your spiritual fervor left? Do you need a boost in your body and spirit?

Obeying and living by God's principles produces life and health. Just as we exercise to strengthen our bodies, we must use our spiritual muscles to attain the strength, peace, and prosperity we all need and desire.

An ancient proverb reads: "He who has health has hope; and he who has hope has everything." As we pray, read, and meditate on God's Word, we increase our spiritual stamina. Although our circumstances may not change, the Lord gives us a new perspective filled with the hope and assurance that we may have lacked before. Exercising our faith produces character and a stronger foundation of trust in the Lord.

Consider this: Medicine left in the cabinet too long loses its potency; masking tape loses its adhesiveness with time; old paint hardens in the can. So when was the last time you shook out the old bones and got moving? A workout for the body and spirit may be just the medicine you need!

—Tina Krause

Hope is like a magnet that draws

you toward your goal.

—H. Norman Wright

Hope deferred makes the heart sick,
but a longing fulfilled is a tree of life.

PROVERBS 13:12 NIV

Joy

Though you have not seen [Jesus],
you love him; and even though you do not see him now,
you believe in him and are filled with an inexpressible and
glorious joy, for you are receiving the end result
of your faith, the salvation of your souls.

1 PETER 1 : 8 – 9 NIV

Accepting the Gift

Lord, You know that sometimes I reject Your promises. When I am really lonely and depressed, nothing seems to make me feel better. I know You are with me; I know You care when no one else cares—but some days even that is not enough. The fault is in me, not in You. On days like that, remind me that although Your promises are free for the taking, I still need to accept them, to claim them, and then to live in faith that they are mine. No gift is truly ours until we open it and accept it in thankfulness and joy.

—Toni Sortor

Joy Is Jesus

As children we find joy in the smallest things: a rose in bloom, a ladybug at rest, the circles a pebble makes when dropped in water. Then somewhere between pigtails and pantyhose our joy wanes and eventually evaporates in the desert of difficulties.

But when we find Jesus, "all things become new" as the Bible promises, and once again, we view the world through a child's eyes. Excitedly, we experience the "inexpressible and glorious joy" that salvation brings.

We learn that God's joy isn't based on our circumstances; rather, its roots begin with the seed of God's Word planted in our hearts. Suddenly, our hearts spill over with joy, knowing that God loves and forgives us and that He is in complete control of our lives. We have joy because we know this world is not our permanent home and a mansion awaits us in glory.

Joy comes as a result of whom we trust, not in what we have. Joy is Jesus.

—Tina Krause

To be a joy-bearer and a joy-giver says everything,

for in our life, if one is joyful, it means that one is

faithfully living for God, and that nothing else counts;

and if one gives joy to others, one is doing God's work;

with joy without and joy within, all is well.

—Janet Erskine Stuart

"Do not grieve, for the joy of the Lord is your strength."

NEHEMIAH 8:10 NIV

Joy

Lord, You are my joy. Knowing You gives me gladness and strength. As my heart's shield, You protect and keep me from harm. Help me to face the future with joy. Fill me with Your good pleasures so I may bring enjoyment to my surroundings—at home, at work, and in my ministry. Help me to laugh more and smile often as I reflect on Your goodness. In Your presence, Lord, is fullness of joy.

—Jackie M. Johnson

Those who sow in tears shall reap in joy.

PSALM 126:5 NKJV

Where the soul is full of peace and joy,

outward surroundings and circumstances

are of comparatively little account.

—Hannah Whitall Smith

For the promise is unto you, and to your children,
and to all that are afar off, even as many as
the LORD *our God shall call.*

ACTS 2:39 KJV

Desert Flower

Friday dawned gloomy and overcast. *A fitting end to a miserable week,* Cheryl thought. Her husband had wrecked the car, and her daughter had broken her thumb in a tumble at school. A beloved friend had been diagnosed with an aggressive form of uterine cancer.

As Cheryl stared at a sky the color of bruises, she blinked back tears and fell to her knees. Second Timothy 4:6 (NIV) came to mind: "I am already being poured out like a drink offering." She could relate to Paul's expression of helplessness. Cheryl felt empty. She cried out to the Lord; then she just cried.

And a strange thing happened. A sensation of warmth started in her toes and spread throughout her body, infusing her with something totally unexpected—joy! She enjoyed a refreshing time of praise-filled fellowship with the renewer of her soul.

Not to be confused with happiness, joy is not dependent on external circumstances. It's a Holy Spirit-inspired mystery that defies all reason. During the times we should be downcast or depressed, the joy of the Lord bolsters us like a life preserver in a tumultuous sea.

Living joyfully is not denying reality. We all have hurts in our lives. But even in the midst of our parched desert times, our heavenly Father reaches in with gentle fingers to lift and sustain us.

—Debora M. Coty

Shouting for Joy!

Your hands created the heavens and the earth. You breathed upon Adam and gave him life. Everything that was created was created through Your Son Jesus Christ. The trees, the earth, the waters, and the creatures clap their hands in praise to You. This is the day that You have made! I will rejoice and be glad in it as I shout Your name to the heavens!

—Donna K. Maltese

Joy is not the fruit of "favorable" circumstances.

Rather, it's the outpouring of a contented heart.

—Wendy Widder

Be glad in the Lord *and rejoice, you righteous;*

and shout for joy, all you upright in heart!

PSALM 32:11 NKJV

Give Me Joy

Lord, Your words are right and true; they bring joy to my heart. I need more joy in my life. Happiness comes and goes, but joy is deep and lasting. This world can take so much out of me with the cares of the day, pressures from my job, and commitments I've made. I need Your true joy despite my circumstances and my feelings. Your commands illuminate me so I can sing Your praises and live revitalized each day. Thank You for Your joy, Lord.

—Jackie M. Johnson

Joy in the Ride

What if we viewed life as an adventurous bicycle ride? With our destination in focus, we would pedal forward, but not so swiftly as to overlook the beauty and experiences that God planted along the way.

We would note the tenacity of a wildflower in bloom despite its unlikely location for growth. We would contemplate God's mercy and savor the brilliance of a rainbow that illuminated a once-blackened sky.

At our halfway point, we would relax from the journey, finding a spot in life's shade to refresh and replenish ourselves for the return trip. We wouldn't just ride; we would explore, pausing along the way to inhale the fresh air and scent of wildflowers.

In life, however, sometimes the road gets rough, and we are forced to take sharp turns. When that happens, we miss the beauty that surrounds us. But if we savor the ride and keep moving forward despite the bumps in the road, then "flowers and singing and joy" will follow.

So when your legs grow weary and your pathway seems long, brace yourself, board your bike, and keep on pedaling. Joy awaits you just around the bend.

—Tina Krause

Love

Jesus replied: " 'Love the Lord your God with all your heart and with all your soul and with all your mind.' This is the first and greatest commandment. And the second is like it: 'Love your neighbor as yourself.' "

MATTHEW 22:37–39 NIV

Working for God's Glory

In the end, Father, You will be the judge of my lifetime of work, and I know You don't care if I work behind a cash register or an oak desk with a five-line telephone. It's not what I do that matters, but how I do it. Am I a cheerful worker? Am I an honest worker? Am I a worker whose love for You is evident in what I say and how I treat my fellow workers? Do I care more for my brothers and sisters than for my next paycheck? I am Your ambassador, Lord, and every day I try to show Your love to those who do not know You. I pray that when the time comes, You will find me worthy.

—Toni Sortor

Convenient Love

Christians have been given two assignments: Love God and love each other.

People say love is a decision. Sounds simple enough, right? The fact is that telling others we love them and showing that love are two very different realities. Let's face it—some people are harder to love than others. Even loving and serving God seem easier on a less stressful day.

Think about convenience stores. They're everywhere. Why? Because along the journey people need things. It's nearly impossible to take a long road trip without stopping. Whether it's gas to fill our vehicles, a quick snack, or a drink to quench thirsty lips, everyone needs something. Gas station owners realize this—and we should, too.

It may not always be convenient to love God when the to-do list stretches on forever or when a friend asks us for a favor that takes more time than we want to give. But God's love is available 24/7. He never puts us on hold or doles out love in rationed amounts. He never takes a day off, and His love is plentiful.

— Kate E. Schmelzer

After the verb "to love". . ."to help" is the

most beautiful verb in the world.

—Bertha von Suttner

Yet in all these things we are more than

conquerors through Him who loved us.

Hold My Hand

Often I am like a little child in a big toy store, running from aisle to aisle and asking for everything that looks good. Sometimes You grant me my wish; other times You say no. Like a loving parent, You hold me by the hand so I don't get lost in the store, just as my mother always did. Like my mother, You point out when my wishes are poorly made or too expensive for my soul. I admit that once in a while I have a temper tantrum, disputing Your guidance and wanting my own way, but You have never been wrong. Thank You for Your love and patience, for I will always need Your guidance.

—Toni Sortor

We love Him because He first loved us.

Love comforteth like sunshine after rain.

—William Shakespeare

Hatred stirs up conflict, but love covers over all wrongs.

PROVERBS 10:12 NIV

Out of Egypt

"When Israel was a child, I loved him, and out of Egypt I called my son." When we think of these words from Hosea 11:1 (NIV), it is usually in connection to Jesus, as God called Him out of Egypt after Herod's death. But read the verse after it, and you will discover God's condemnation of His wandering people. Though God called Israel with love, they turned aside from Him to pagan worship.

Scripture often holds similar surprises. An uplifting verse is followed by one that speaks of deep sin. God's promises and humanity's sin run together in entwined messages.

Isn't that just the way the Christian life is? God's merciful thread runs through our pain-filled, erroneous lives. Like a bright, gold line, it brightens our existence and begins to turn us from sin-filled ore to bright, pure gold.

For not only did God call His Son from Egypt; He calls us, too, to leave behind the darkness of sin and live in His holiness. His love strips evil from us and brings us into close relationship to Him.

God has called you out of Egypt because He loves you. Love Him in return.

—Pamela McQuade

A New Beginning

Lord, now that I am devoted to You heart and soul, I am a new creation. Thank You for washing away my old ways of thinking and behaving, and for empowering me to live a new life. Your love changes me! Help me to live this new life with wisdom, making the right choices. Give me the courage to love the way You love. Teach me Your ways as we journey together on this path toward heaven. . .toward home.

—Jackie M. Johnson

Nothing is inexorable but love.

— George MacDonald

He who does not love does not know God, for God is love.

1 JOHN 4:8 NKJV

Love One Another

What an example of love You give us, Jesus! You laid down Your life for everyone—even while we were still sinners. Fill me with that kind of love, Lord, that self-sacrificing love. So often, my thoughts seem to be all about me and what I want. Help me to change that by following Your example. I want to be like You, serving others with compassion, understanding, patience, and kindness. Give me that power, that longing, to love those who love me, those who hate me, and those who are indifferent to me.

—Donna K. Maltese

More Than Words Can Say

Silence—for many people it can be quite uncomfortable. Televisions, stereos, and iPods fill the void. Incessant conversation is the norm. Noise must permeate the air. What is it about silence that agitates us so? Perhaps pondering our own thoughts is frightening. Maybe we need constant reassurance from others that we are not alone.

We may desperately desire to hear from God, yet sometimes He chooses to remain silent. How do we interpret His silence? Do we become fearful, uneasy, or confused? We may feel that He has abandoned us, but this is not true. When God is silent, His love is still present. When God is silent, He is still in control. When God is silent, He is still communicating. Do not miss it. His silence speaks volumes.

Most couples who are deeply in love do not have to exchange words to communicate their love. They can experience contentment and unwavering trust in the midst of silence. The presence of their loved one is enough. That is what God desires in our love relationship with Him. He wants us to abide in His presence. Silence prohibits distraction. As we continue to trust Him amid the silence, we learn that His presence is all we need. God has promised that He will never leave us nor forsake us. Believe Him. Trust Him. His presence is enough.

—Julie Rayburn

Prayer

Hear my prayer, O LORD, and let my cry come to You.

PSALM 102:1 NKJV

Elisabeth

Zacharias and Elisabeth had waited years for a child, and now they both were old, well past the age for bearing children, no matter how much they wanted one. Then Gabriel, Your messenger, appeared to Zacharias with the good news that the son Elisabeth would bear would prepare the way for the coming of Your Son. Father, sometimes it seems my deepest desires will never bear fruit, no matter how much I pray. I go on with my life, but there is an emptiness in my heart that only You can fill. I know not all prayers are answered, but many are, so I continue to petition You, for You are my hope.

—Toni Sortor

Trust Test

Have you had days when your prayers seemed to hit the ceiling and bounce back? Does God seem distant for no reason you're aware of? Chances are good that if you've been a Christian for more than a short time, you've experienced this.

The psalmist experienced it as pain and suffering became his lot. At night insomnia plagued him. During his tired days, enemies taunted him. His was a weary life, and in earthly terms, he hardly could see the outcome.

But once the psalmist described his plight, his psalm turned in a new direction, glorifying God. Suddenly, life wasn't so bad anymore, because he trusted in the One who would save him.

When prayer hits the ceiling, it's time to remind ourselves of God's greatness, not complain about what we think He hasn't done. As we face trials that threaten to undo us, let's remind ourselves that He has not forgotten us, and our ultimate security is never at risk.

As we feel the dangers of life, let's trust that God is still listening to our prayers. He will never fail us. All He asks is that our reliance on Him remains firm. At the right hour, we'll feel His love again.

—Pamela McQuade

I have been driven many times to my knees

by the overwhelming conviction that

I had absolutely no other place to go.

—Abraham Lincoln

"Which of you, if your son asks for bread, will give him a stone?"

MATTHEW 7:9 NIV

Prayer

Lord, Your house is a house of prayer for all nations. Thank You for the gift of prayer, our two-way conversation with You. Help us to make prayer a priority every day. Lead us as we lift up our adoration, confession, thanksgiving, and supplication—of asking You for everything we need. May we be intercessors, praying for other people and their needs. May we bask in the glory of Your light so we can reflect the Father's heart to all we meet. Lord, teach us to pray.

—Jackie M. Johnson

Let my prayer be set before You as incense,

the lifting up of my hands as the evening sacrifice.

PSALM 141:2 NKJV

Pray, and let God worry.

— Martin Luther

I call on you, my God, for you will answer me;

turn your ear to me and hear my prayer.

PSALM 17:6 NIV

Available 24/7

No one is available to take your call at this time, so leave a message and we will return your call—or not—if we feel like it. . .and only between the hours of 4:00 and 4:30 p.m. Thank you for calling. Have a super day!

We've all felt the frustration of that black hole called voice mail. It is rare to reach a real, honest-to-goodness, breathing human being the first time we dial a telephone number.

Fortunately, our God is always available. He can be reached at any hour of the day or night and every day of the year—including weekends and holidays! When we pray, we don't have to worry about disconnections, hang-ups, or poor reception. We will never be put on hold or our prayers diverted to another department.

The Bible assures us that God is eager to hear our petitions and that He welcomes our prayers of thanksgiving. The psalmist David wrote of God's response to those who put their trust in Him: "He will call on me, and I will answer him" (Psalm 91:15 NIV). David had great confidence that God would hear his prayers. And we can, too!

—Austine Keller

Perseverance in Prayer

I feel like I've been praying forever for a situation that does not seem to be changing, Lord. I feel like Job: Here I am on my knees in prayer while the entire world dissolves around me. But I know that You are in control. You know all things. So once again, I lift my concern up to You, confident that You will handle the situation in Your timing.

—Donna K. Maltese

Faith thrives in an atmosphere of prayer.

— E. M. Bounds

Therefore I tell you, whatever you ask for in prayer,
believe that you have received it, and it will be yours.

MARK 11:24 NIV

Making Prayer a Priority

Lord, I feel like a withered plant with dry, brown leaves. Help me connect with You in prayer so I can grow strong and healthy—inside and out—like a vibrant green tree. You are my source of living water. Teach me to be still, to listen, to absorb what You want to reveal to me in this time of inward filling. In this holy conversation, may I find freedom, peace, and joy—and a closer walk with You.

—Jackie M. Johnson

Peace through Prayer

Some days it is easy to be thankful. We nearly bubble over with thanksgiving. These are mountaintop days—a graduation day, a wedding, or a reunion with old friends. The day comes to a close, and we whisper a prayer. It flows easily off the tongue. "Thank You, God," we say, "for a perfect day."

There are days when thankfulness is not as natural, not as easy. These are valley days—in the hospital room, at the graveside, or when we are distraught about a relationship or work issue. It is in these times that the Father wants us to give Him our burdens through prayer. It seems impossible to be thankful for the pain, the confusion, or the longings in our lives. We can be thankful, though, that we have a loving heavenly Father who stands ready to help.

The peace of God cannot be explained. It cannot be bought. The world cannot give it to us. But when we release our cares to the Lord in prayer, His peace washes over us and fills our hearts and minds. What a comfort is the peace of God when we find ourselves in the valley.

—Emily Biggers

When we feel least like praying is the time

when we most need to pray.

— R. A. Torrey

Rejoice always, pray without ceasing,
in everything give thanks; for this is the will
of God in Christ Jesus for you.

1 Thessalonians 5:16—18 NKJV

Strength

By his divine power, God has given us everything
we need for living a godly life.

2 PETER 1:3 NLT

Our Source of Strength

On my own, I am rarely as strong as I need to be, Lord. Sickness weakens me; cares and worry tire my mind and make me less productive than I want to be. Old age will eventually defeat my body. Even when I am physically fit, I know there is weakness in me. But You promise that I will be able to continue in Your way as long as I have faith, and I trust Your promises. Make me stronger every day, Lord, no matter how heavy my burdens may be. Show me all the good You have done for the faithful throughout history and give me some of Your strength when my own fails. Let my dependence on You turn weakness into strength.

—Toni Sortor

Hold On

Life is the moment—the here and now—yet we spend much of our time outside of that moment worried about, focused on, and trying to figure out the next hour, the next day, week, or month. Where will the money for this come from? Where will I be next year? How will my children turn out?

Life comes at us fast—and we have to take each challenge as it comes. Sometimes there are so many variables to juggle that we just want to give up. Don't let go—but hold on. The enemy of your soul wants you to quit. You've gotten this far in your faith believing that God will keep His promises and help you reach your destiny.

When you don't think you can take another step—

don't! Just hold on. Tomorrow will give you a fresh start with the strength you need to go a little farther and hold on a little longer. Take a deep breath, get a fresh grasp on your faith, and don't let go. God will help you get to your dream.

—Shanna D. Gregor

If God sends us on stony paths,

he provides strong shoes.

—CORRIE TEN BOOM

"I will make a pathway through the wilderness.
I will create rivers in the dry wasteland."

ISAIAH 43:19 NLT

Finding Strength

Lord, I am tired and weary. Infuse me with life, energy, and joy again. I thank You for being my strength and my delight. I don't have to look to a bowl of ice cream or the compliments of a friend to fill me up on the inside. Steady and constant, You are my source; You are the One who fills me. Sustain me, Lord, with the power of Your love, so I can live my life refreshed and renewed.

—Jackie M. Johnson

In God is my salvation and my glory;
the rock of my strength, and my refuge, is in God.

PSALM 62:7 NKJV

Our strength grows out of our weaknesses.

—Ralph Waldo Emerson

I can do all things through Christ

which strengtheneth me.

Mountains out of Molehills

Some days mountains of work are piled in front of us. Whether they consist of schoolwork, diapers, dirty laundry, business reports, or all of the above, the height of such tasks can sometimes seem to be overwhelming. We don't even know where to begin. Immediately the enemy begins whispering in our ears, "Good luck trying to get all that done. You don't have a chance. And if you try to rush through it, no one will be happy with the results. Especially not you."

These are the times when we need to take stock of the situation. First things first. Don't panic! Take a deep breath. Tell yourself that you can do all things with Christ's strength (see Philippians 4:13). You have God's word on it. Send up a prayer for strength. Then just simply do the next thing. Take the first step.

Although situations sometimes seem impossible, we have a God—a great big, mighty God—who makes a way in the wilderness for us. He can move mountains. Nothing will stop Him from helping us— except maybe ourselves and a negative mind-set. Do not doubt. But take that first step forward, knowing He will make a way where there seems to be no way.

—Donna K. Maltese

Needing Encouragement

Lord, I need encouragement. Will You please inspire my heart and strengthen me in everything I say and do? I need Your truth to lift my spirit and help me soar. Let me be like an eagle that glides on the wind. Give me the courage and energy I need to keep going even when I'm weary.

—Jackie M. Johnson

Since God Himself is a steadfast Rock, the foundation

of all certitude and steadfastness, it must be by faith or

holding fast to God that man can become steadfast.

—Andrew Murray

God is our refuge and strength,
a very present help in trouble.

PSALM 46:1 KJV

Strength in Weakness

It's a paradox, but it is Your truth. When I am weak, I am strong because Your strength is made perfect in my weakness. Because You are in my life, I can rest in You. With Your loving arms around me, I am buoyed in spirit, soul, and body. When I am with You there is peace and comfort.

—Donna K. Maltese

Restoration

Have you ever felt that God abandoned you? Have the difficulties in your life pressed you to physical and mental exhaustion? Do you feel your labor is in vain and no one appreciates the sacrifices you have made?

When Elijah fled for his life in fear of Jezebel's wrath, depression and discouragement tormented him. Exhausted, he prayed for God to take his life, and then he fell asleep. When he awoke, God sent an angel with provisions to strengthen his weakened body. Only then was he able to hear God's revelation that provided the direction and assistance he needed.

God hears our pleas even when He seems silent. The problem is that we cannot hear Him because of physical and mental exhaustion. Rest is key to our restoration. Just when the prophet thought he could go on no longer, God provided the strength, peace, and encouragement to continue. He does the same for us today. When we come to the end of our rope, God ties a knot. And like Elijah, God will do great things in and through us, if we will just hold on.

—Tina Krause

Trials

Give thanks to the LORD, *for he is good;*

his love endures forever.

PSALM 107:1 NIV

My Defense

No matter what befalls me in my lifetime, my defenses remain strong in times of trouble. They are not the defenses of an armed force, as necessary as that may be from time to time; they are the safety of Your promises and the assurance of Your mighty protection. Times do get difficult in this world. Conflict is always with us in some part of the world, and conflict brings tension, but tension should never become fear or the inability to enjoy this wonderful world You have given us. I pray You will always be my strength, my rock, my salvation. Hear me when I call to You for help, for I know You love me.

—Toni Sortor

Steadfast Love

When the sea of life batters us, it's easy to forget the Lord's goodness. Caught up in our own storms, tunnel vision afflicts us as we view the troubles before us and may doubt the Lord whom we serve. Though we might not consciously separate ourselves from Him, deep inside we fear He won't act to save us—or that He won't act in time.

That's a good time to stop and give thanks to God, who never stops being good or ends His love for us. Our situations change, our love fails, but God never varies. He entirely controls all creation, and His character never changes. The darkest circumstances we face will not last eternally. Life moves on and alters. But God never deserts us.

Even when our troubles seem to be in control, they aren't. God has not changed, and our doubts cannot make alteration in Him. If we allow faith to take control, we will realize that and turn again to Him.

Facing troubles? Give thanks to the Lord. He is good. He hasn't deserted you, no matter what you face, and His goodness will never end. He won't fail us.

—Pamela McQuade

By trials God is shaping us for higher things.

—Henry Ward Beecher

Cast your burden upon the LORD
and He will sustain you;
He will never allow the righteous to be shaken.

PSALM 55:22 NASB

Overcoming the World

Lord, You warned the disciples that the path lying before them was both steep and dangerous. During the course of bringing Your Word to the world, they would become the first martyrs of the church, hounded and persecuted to death on all sides. Still, You urged them to be happy in this life. Although the world would treat them wickedly, You had overcome the world, and Your salvation was theirs forever. The power of the world is no match for You, and because of Your sacrifice, all it can do to us is kill the body and free the soul for eternal life with You.

—Toni Sortor

Count it all joy when you fall into various trials,
knowing that the testing of your faith produces patience.

JAMES 1:2–3 NKJV

Trials are medicines which our gracious and wise Physician prescribes because we need them; and He proportions the frequency and weight of them to what the case requires. Let us trust His skill and thank Him for His prescription.

— Isaac Newton

These things I have spoken unto you,

that in me ye might have peace.

In the world ye shall have tribulation:

but be of good cheer; I have overcome the world.

JOHN 16:33 KJV

Giving God Your Burdens

When we have a problem, our first thought is to contact a friend. In our world today, with so many technological advances, it is easy to communicate even with people who are far away. Just a hundred years ago, people waited days to receive a message from another town!

Certainly God desires that we help to bear one another's burdens and that we seek wise counsel. The trouble is that in doing so, often we fail to take our burdens to the One who can do something about them. We are called to release our cares to our heavenly Father. A cause with an effect is implied in Psalm 55:22—If you cast your burden on Him, then He will sustain you.

Sustain is defined by Webster as a verb meaning "to strengthen or support physically or mentally" or "to bear the weight of an object." Does it sound inviting to have the sovereign God of the universe strengthen and support you? Would it help if He bore the weight of your current trial? Our sovereign God is there when heartaches are taking their toll. He doesn't have a cell phone or an e-mail address, but He is always just a prayer away.

—Emily Biggers

Joy Despite Trials

Lord, it seems odd to consider trials a joyful thing. But I pray that my challenges in life, these times of testing, will lead me to greater perseverance. May that perseverance finish its work so I will be mature and complete, on my way to wholeness. I ask for wisdom and Your perspective as I seek joy in life's challenges— and the better times that will come my way.

—Jackie M. Johnson

You do not understand what troubles means;

you have hardly sipped the cup of trouble;

you have only had a drop or two,

but Jesus drunk the dregs.

—Charles Spurgeon

Who shall separate us from the love of Christ?

Shall trouble or hardship or persecution

or famine or nakedness or danger or sword? . . .

No, in all these things we are more than

conquerors through him who loved us.

ROMANS 8:35, 37 NIV

Blessings amid the Storm

Lord, when I look back on all the ways You have blessed me and continue to bless me, even through these trials, I am awed and thankful. As You have delivered me in the past, deliver me again from the troubles before me. Lift the burdens off my sagging shoulders. I leave them at the foot of Your cross, as instructed. Thank You, Lord. I love You so much. Now with each breath I take, I relax and enter into Your rest.

—Donna K. Maltese

Expect Trouble

Why do bad things happen to good people? It is an age-old question. Sometimes we expect God to surround us with an invisible shield that keeps us from all harm and disease, all hurt and disappointment. As nice as this might sound, it is simply not how life works. Christians are not exempt from trials.

In the Gospel of John, we read that Christ told his followers to expect trouble in this world. The good news is that we do not have to face it alone. When trials come, remember that Jesus has overcome this world. Through Him, we, too, are overcomers. Draw upon the promise that through Christ you can do all things. The children's song says it this way: "Jesus loves me, this I know, for the Bible tells me so. Little ones to

Him belong. They are weak, but He is strong."

Expect trouble, but refuse to let it defeat you. Trials strengthen our faith and our character. No one gets excited about a trial, yet we can be assured that God is still in control even when trouble comes our way.

—Emily Biggers

Wisdom

"My sheep listen to my voice;
I know them, and they follow me."

JOHN 10:27 NIV

Looking in All the Wrong Places

Embracing wisdom is not difficult for a child of God; finding it is harder. In our search for wisdom, we often chase after it in the wrong places. The evening news may give us the facts, but its interpretation of the facts is often flawed. Professors try to build wisdom through the teachings of knowledge, but a wise student carefully evaluates any conclusions a teacher draws from the facts. Only You are the perfect source of wisdom, Father. You give it to us liberally when we ask for it, never considering us stupid or leading us astray. You have given us Your Word as the best schoolbook of true wisdom.

—Toni Sortor

Listening vs. Talking

It has been said that the Lord gave us two ears and one mouth for a reason: We need to listen twice as much as we speak. However, talking seems to come easier for most of us. Our interaction with others becomes the model for our relationship with the Lord. We can become so busy talking to Him during our prayer time that we forget He has important wisdom to impart to us!

Jesus is our Good Shepherd. As His sheep, we have the ability to distinguish His voice. But are we taking the time to listen? It seems much of our prayer time is devoted to reciting our wish list to God. When we stop and think about it, doesn't God already know our needs before we utter one word? We need to learn to listen more instead of dominating the conversation. God is the One with the answers. He knows all things and possesses the wisdom we yearn for.

Learning to listen takes time. Do not be afraid to sit in silence before the Lord. Read His Word. He will speak softly to your heart. He will impart truth to your hungry soul. He will guide you on the path you should take. Listen.

— Julie Rayburn

A loving heart is the truest wisdom.

—Charles Dickens

But the wisdom that is from above is first pure,
then peaceable, gentle, and easy to be intreated,
full of mercy and good fruits, without partiality,
and without hypocrisy.

JAMES 3:17 KJV

Walking in Wisdom

Lord, please keep me from the foolishness of sin. I ask for wisdom and discernment to make wise choices in my life. When I'm tempted, give me the strength to flee it. When I am uncertain, help me to know the right course of action. When I need good ideas, enlighten my mind with creativity and intelligence. You know everything, Lord—may I walk in Your wisdom and learn Your ways.

—Jackie M. Johnson

The excellence of knowledge is that wisdom
gives life to those who have it.

ECCLESIASTES 7:12 NKJV

God, grant me the serenity to accept the things I
cannot change, the courage to change the things I can,
and the wisdom to know the difference.

—Reinhold Niebuhr

But to those who are called, both Jews and Greeks,
Christl the power of God and the wisdom of God.

Losing Interest

Every season of dangerous weather brings uncertainty. Normally meteorologists can track a storm's progress, but even if everyone is told to evacuate early, not every possession can be taken or protected. The aftermath of hurricanes, tornadoes, floods, and other natural disasters proves that possessions can be gone in seconds.

Some people stake their identities in acquiring possessions. Others live to make names for themselves. Even living for family members and friends can feel unsatisfying and empty.

Having money and possessions isn't wrong. Even having high-priced possessions isn't wrong. But there is something missing when our desire for wealth outweighs our desire for God. We may hold on too tightly to things that don't have eternal value and not cling closely enough to the One who does.

God has asked us to use wisdom as we work for Him. Wisdom plans for the future, but it also recognizes that even plans fail. Finances and storms come and go. Our trust in God can be a firm anchor.

— Kate E. Schmelzer

Walking in God's Wisdom

Lord, I want to do what You have created me to do. I come to You today, seeking Your direction for my life. I have my own ideas of how You want me to serve You, to enlarge Your kingdom here on earth, to provide for myself, my family, and my church. But I need Your wisdom. Which route should I take? When shall I begin? How shall I go? Lead me, Lord, into the waters You have chartered for my life.

— Donna K. Maltese

The wisdom of this age is folly in view of eternity.

—John Piper

How much better to get wisdom than gold,

to get insight rather than silver!

PROVERBS 16:16 NIV

The Wisdom of Peace

Lord, please plant Your wisdom in me like seeds in the soil. Each one is a gift from heaven. Help me cultivate each one and learn to follow Your ways. They are pure, peaceloving, considerate, submissive, full of mercy and good fruit, impartial, and sincere. May I be a person who sows in peace and raises a harvest of righteousness. As I look to Your Word for growth, teach me to meditate on it and apply it to my life.

—Jackie M. Johnson

Realistic Expectations

Working, cleaning, cooking, attending meetings, calling people, going places—life is full of business, things we have to accomplish. We often make lists to help us remember what we need to do and when. At the end of the day, we can look back and see what we have finished and what is left to juggle into tomorrow's schedule.

If the unexpected happens, our schedule is thrown off. We struggle to find the time to do everything we have listed to do. We become stressed. Sleeping becomes difficult. Our health suffers. Friends and relatives may note a change in our demeanor.

God worked hard to create the wonderful world around us, yet He did so with wisdom and proper timing. He didn't do everything in one day. Instead, He had a plan and accomplished all He needed to do in that time frame.

Consider what is important in life. Start your day with God; then list your agenda in order of importance. As we let God lead, His wisdom will make us have realistic expectations. Our well-being and attitude will improve.

—Nancy Farrier